David Roberts R. A.

Saint Catherine's Monastery, Sinai, Egypt

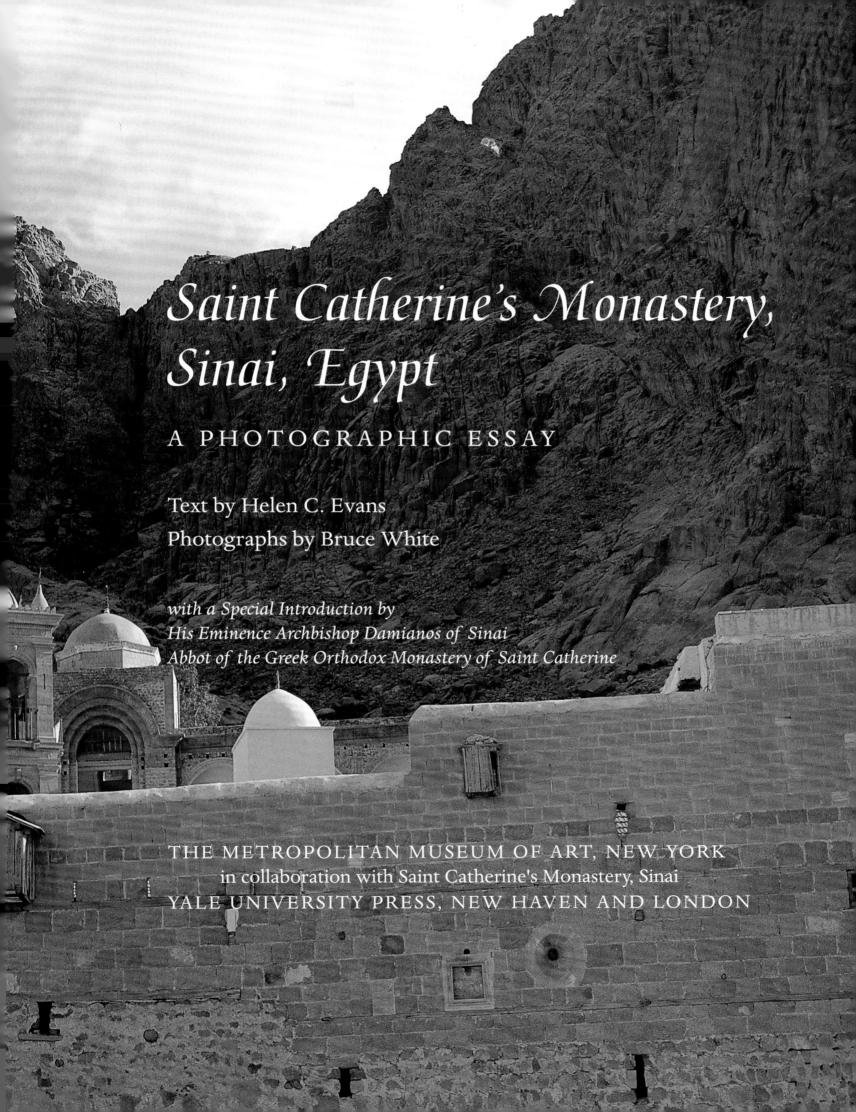

Saint Catherine's Monastery, Sinai, Egypt

A PHOTOGRAPHIC ESSAY

Text by Helen C. Evans

Photographs by Bruce White

*with a Special Introduction by
His Eminence Archbishop Damianos of Sinai
Abbot of the Greek Orthodox Monastery of Saint Catherine*

THE METROPOLITAN MUSEUM OF ART, NEW YORK
in collaboration with Saint Catherine's Monastery, Sinai
YALE UNIVERSITY PRESS, NEW HAVEN AND LONDON

Published by The Metropolitan Museum of Art, New York

Copyright © 2004 by The Metropolitan Museum of Art, New York

John P. O'Neill, Editor in Chief

Ellen Shultz, Editor

Bruce Campbell, Designer

Gwen Roginsky and Jill Pratzon, Production

Minjee Cho, Desktop Publishing

The photographs on pages 6, 30, 37, 50, and 92–93 are by Monk Daniel Sinaites.

Library of Congress Cataloging-in-Publication Data

Evans, Helen C.

    Saint Catherine's Monastery, Sinai, Egypt: a photographic essay / text by Helen C. Evans; photographs by Bruce White; with a special introduction by His Eminence Archbishop Damianos of Sinai.

       p. cm.

    ISBN 1-58839-109-4 (hardcover)—ISBN 1-58839-110-8 (pbk.)—ISBN 0-300-10279-8 (Yale University Press)

    1. Saint Catherine (Monastery : Mount Sinai) 2. Saint Catherine (Monastery : Mount Sinai)—Pictorial works. I. White, Bruce M. II. Title.

    BX387.E93 2004

    271'.819531—dc22   2003026718

Cover/jacket: Saint Catherine's Monastery, Sinai, Egypt.

Endpapers: Saint Catherine's Monastery. Print by David Roberts, R.A.

Title page: View of Saint Catherine's Monastery from outside the walls.

Printed and bound in Spain

Contents

Mount Sinai, with its peak illuminated by sunlight.

Introduction

"He took up the monastic yoke in Mount Sinai, and, I think, by the visible nature of the place itself, he was impelled and guided towards the invisible God."

THE WORDS of Daniel, Abbot of Raitho, quoted above, from his vita of Saint John Climacus, Abbot of Sinai in the seventh century, were included as an introduction to Saint John's immortal book *The Ladder of Divine Ascent*. It truly can be said that the "visible nature" of Sinai impels and guides the soul "towards the invisible God."

The terrain on the highest reaches of the Sinai Peninsula consists of barren and desert land. Red granite mountains soar upward toward the sky. This is a landscape of narrow valleys and precipitous cliffs. The sky is a proverbial deep blue; the sunlight is brilliant. The air is remarkably clear, and objects at a distance look quite close. Yet, Mount Sinai is known and revered throughout the world not only for its scenic grandeur but because it was at this place, over three thousand years ago, that God revealed himself in a special way. It was here that the prophet Moses beheld the bush that burned but was not consumed, and heard the voice of God: "Moses, Moses, draw not nigh hither: put off thy shoes from off thy feet, for the place whereon thou standest is holy ground." At the peak of Sinai he witnessed the glory of God, and received the Tablets of the Law. On another occasion, it is written of Moses and Aaron and all the elders of Israel that ". . . they saw the God of Israel: and there was under His feet as it were a paved work of a sapphire stone, and as it were the body of heaven in his clearness."

The prophet Moses remains the paradigm for all who seek to enter into the very presence of God. As Saint Gregory of Nyssa wrote in his *Life of Moses*, "In the same way that Moses on that occasion attained to this knowledge, so now does everyone who, like him, divests himself of the earthly covering and looks to the light shining from the bramble bush, that is (as the Gospel says) the true light and the truth itself."[1]

For over seventeen centuries, those who were eager to take up the yoke of obedience and to make the arduous ascent to spiritual heights have been drawn to this holy place. The fathers of the desert were very strenuous, giving themselves over to prayer and fasting, setting aside their own will in all things in their longing to conform to the Divine will. Yet, from these austerities and this zeal came gentleness, sensitivity, earnest care to avoid giving offense, and profound humility.

In this vast solitude, a multitude attained the heights of sanctity. While the greater number, surely, are known only to God, many have been glorified by God, and are venerated as saints throughout the Orthodox Church. They have left their words and example as guideposts, and these have been the inspiration for all who seek to follow them. Saint Gregory of Sinai, for one, has written: "Christ is the capstone uniting us with Himself. He is the pearl of great price: it is this for which the monk seeks when he plunges into the depths of stillness and it is this for which he sells all his own desires through obedience to the commandments, so that he may acquire it even in this life."[2] As he explains:

> *The physical eye perceives the outward or literal sense of things and from it derives sensory images. The eye of the soul (the* nous*), once purified and reestablished in its pristine state, perceives God and from Him derives divine images. Instead of a book, it has the Spirit; instead of a pen, mind and tongue—"my tongue is a pen," says the psalmist; and instead of ink, light. So plunging the mind into the light that it becomes light, the eye of the soul, guided by the Spirit, inscribes the inner meaning of things in the pure hearts of those who listen. Then it grasps the significance of the statement that the faithful "shall be taught of God," and that through the Spirit God "teaches man knowledge."*[3]

The monks of old passed their lives at services and in prayer. They wrote and copied manuscripts, to serve as inspiration or for use in worship. They painted icons, witnesses of the Incarnation, hieratic visions of the heavenly kingdom. The Holy Monastery also received gifts from pilgrims, or from distant lands, including manuscripts, vestments, embroideries, chalices, and other ecclesiastical works of art.

In recent decades, the modern world has come rushing in. Indeed, no monastery today is as remote as it once was. Saint Catherine's Monastery now receives many pilgrims and visitors each year. They are attracted to this site because of its sanctity, its long history, its scenic beauty, and, perhaps, because of its former inaccessibility. They also come to see and to study the multitude of icons, manuscripts, vestments, embroideries, and other examples of ecclesiastical art, for which the Holy Monastery is justly renowned.

As beautiful and as significant as the icons and manuscripts are, it is important to remember that they were not created solely as works of art but for prayer and worship, and they are best appreciated in that context; at the Holy Monastery, that context has remained intact. Sacred texts and icons still inspire the members of the brotherhood, and icons, vestments, and other ecclesiastical objects continue to be employed in the daily services. While much has changed at Sinai in recent decades, within the sixth-century fortress walls, the cycle of services and the ancient and distilled way of life continue very much as they always have.

The masterful photographs that are featured in this book are by Bruce White, a talented and experienced photographer, who has visited the Sinai on a number of occasions. The strong contrasts of light and shadow in his photographs endow the surrounding mountains with a stark beauty. They include views of remote chapels, of the imposing fortress walls, and of the sixth-century basilica—all of which have stood for centuries in this age-old monastery. There also are photographs of Holy Week and Easter services, and of the celebration of the feast of Saint Catherine, patron saint of the Holy Monastery. The pictures capture the living community at worship and in prayer, and at moments when the monks are joined by a multitude of pilgrims or are occupied with carrying out their daily activities; they are in this world, but not of this world: "The fashion of this world passeth away. . . . Here we have no continuing city, but we seek one to come." Also photographed are the Bedouin,

who have been associated with the Holy Monastery from the sixth century. The Bedouin are Arabic-speaking Muslims with families, while the monks of Sinai are Orthodox Christian monastics whose common language is Greek. Where differences of language, religion, and culture might have caused tensions and discord, there has been, instead, a relationship of deep regard and mutual support between the monks and the Bedouin; each group respects the other, in religious matters above all. This, indeed, sets an important example for those who seek peace in our own times.

A limited number of additional photographs in the following pages have been supplied by the Holy Monastery, from its own archives.

This volume is being published in conjunction with the exhibition "Byzantium: Faith and Power (1261–1557)" at The Metropolitan Museum of Art in spring 2004, and is a sequel to "The Glory of Byzantium: Art and Culture of the Middle Byzantine Era, A.D. 843–1261," held at the Museum in 1997, in which Saint Catherine's Monastery also participated. By contributing to such exhibitions, the Monastery hopes that it will enable all to learn of, to understand, and to appreciate the incomparable spiritual and artistic heritage that has been preserved in the Sinai desert for so many centuries. For those who are able to see the Holy Monastery's icons and manuscripts in this exhibition, this book will be all the more significant, as it presents many of these same objects, as they appear at the Holy Monastery, and clarifies the place they hold in the living community.

We are grateful to Mahrukh Tarapor, Associate Director for Exhibitions; Helen C. Evans, Curator, Department of Medieval Art and The Cloisters; and to all those at The Metropolitan Museum of Art—as well as to Bruce White—who have had a part in bringing this volume to completion. May all who have labored over this book, and all who will read it, receive the grace and blessing of God, which rests upon this holy place.

His Eminence Archbishop Damianos of Sinai
Abbot of the Greek Orthodox Monastery of Saint Catherine

1. *Gregory of Nyssa: The Life of Moses,* translated by Abraham J. Malherbe and Everett Ferguson (New York: Paulist Press, 1978), p. 61.
2. *The Philokalia: The Complete Text,* translated and edited by G. E. H. Palmer, Philip Sherrard, and Kallistos Ware, vol. 4 (London: Faber and Faber, 1995), p. 228.
3. Ibid., pp. 216–17.

Preface

THE IDEA FOR THIS volume originated with my colleague, Mahrukh Tarapor, Associate Director for Exhibitions, during one of her many visits to the Holy Monastery of Saint Catherine, when she realized that no existing book fully captured the relationship between the Monastery and the austere grandeur of the surrounding landscape. In a conversation with Archbishop Damianos, Mahrukh suggested that the Museum would be interested in creating such a publication, and the Metropolitan Museum appreciates greatly his positive response to this proposal.

This present volume marks the latest chapter in the cooperation between the Holy Monastery of Saint Catherine and The Metropolitan Museum of Art, which began some six years ago with the unprecedented loan of some of the Monastery's most important icons to our exhibition "The Glory of Byzantium (843–1261)" in 1997. This collaboration has continued into 2004, with the extraordinarily generous loan of as many as forty icons to the subsequent exhibition "Byzantium: Faith and Power (1261–1557)," which will demonstrate the Monastery's significant role in the later centuries of the Byzantine world. In the years between, the Metropolitan was honored to have advised the Monastery on the design and installation of its Sacristy, a new permanent gallery within its ancient walls where the Monastery's most magnificent works of art are safely displayed for the enjoyment of many visitors worldwide.

In this collection of splendid photographs by Bruce White the Metropolitan Museum has sought to capture both the monumental landscape and the sacred warmth and humanity of the institution, which has stood for more than 1,700 years on land consecrated by the prophet Moses. The essay by Helen C. Evans offers insight into the history of the mountainous terrain and the Monastery through the centuries, including the Monastery's critical role as an outpost of the Byzantine Empire and its Orthodox Church. It is the Museum's special privilege to include in this volume photographs taken by Father Daniel and captions written by Father Justin.

The Metropolitan Museum of Art has participated with the Holy Monastery in the development of this publication with a sense of gratitude and homage to the monks who have guided Saint Catherine's spiritual growth throughout the centuries.

Philippe de Montebello
Director
The Metropolitan Museum of Art

The Holy Monastery of Saint Catherine on the God-trodden Mount Sinai

Helen C. Evans

SURROUNDINGS

Approaching the Holy Monastery of Saint Catherine on the God-trodden Mount Sinai, the desert land-scape yields to low mountains and then to higher and higher ridges. On the road from Cairo, the great oasis at Pharan (modern Feiran) is marked by hundreds of ancient palm trees. In the fourth century, Christianity flourished at this site on the ancient trade routes that crisscrossed the region. Along these routes, goods were carried from India and China into Egypt and up the Mediterranean coast into the Holy Land and beyond.

Nearing the Holy Monastery, the mountains become increasingly steep. At daybreak and at dusk, they seem trans-formed into walls of dark rosy pink or golden orange. A few trees, or bushes, add subtle green tones to the landscape. Camels, or a few herds of goats, may be seen, but it is their Bedouin keepers' brightly colored garb that stands out vividly against the landscape.

Small churches, or hermitages, come into view on nearby mountaintops, signs that one is drawing closer to the moun-tains that house the Holy Monastery. Some of these build-ings may date back to the time of the Nabataean peoples who lived in the area in the first centuries of the Christian era. They are evidence of the sacred respect in which these mountains have been held for centuries—in fact, for long before the birth of Christ.

Opening out at the foot of the large wadi in which the Holy Monastery is located is the plain of El-Raha ("the resting place"). The vast, level plain funnels into an increasingly nar-row, twisting cleft in the mountains, where the massive walls of the fortified Holy Monastery appear. The huge rock faces at either side seem like enormous hands, holding the Holy Monastery in their safe grasp. A long, narrow garden filled with flowering trees and tall, thin cypress plants proves that this site, too, is an oasis—a place to gather water in the arid desert.

It has long been argued that El-Raha is one of the most important sites on the route along which the Old Testament prophet Moses led his people out of Egypt. According to the Book of Exodus 2–3, Moses fled from Egypt after he had killed an Egyptian who had abused a Jewish worker. Escaping the pharaoh's wrath, he came into the Sinai, where he met and married one of the daughters of Jethro. He remained in the region for forty years; then, God appeared to Moses in the Burning Bush and ordered him to return to Egypt to lead his people out of their bondage.

Parting the Red Sea, Moses brought his people out of Egypt and into the Sinai on their way to the Promised Land. For many centuries, the plain of El-Raha has been thought to be where they camped while Moses ascended a great mountain beyond the Holy Monastery, the Jebel Musa, and received the Ten Commandments from God. Those camped out on the plain ordered Moses' brother Aaron to make them idols to worship but when Moses returned from the mountain heights after forty days, he destroyed the idol of the golden calf. A rock near the entrance to the Holy Monastery now is often described as the mold in which the calf was cast (Exodus 14–36).

Nearer to Jebel Musa, a small church marks the presence in the region of the prophet Elias, who is said to have fled to the area after killing the prophets of Baal: "And he arose, and did eat and drink, and went in the strength of that meat forty days and forty nights unto Horeb the mount of God" (I Kings 19: 8). There, God revealed himself, not in earthquake or strong wind or fire, but in "a still small voice" (I Kings 19: 12), or, as the Greek text of the Old Testament relates, "the voice of a gentle breeze."

Christians began to settle in individual hermitages in the region by the third century, in order to be near the biblical sites and to be secure from the persecutions that they received, as an illegal religious minority, in more settled parts of the Roman Empire. In 313, the new Roman emperor Constantine the Great ordered that Christianity be recognized as a legal religion within the empire. Increasing numbers of pilgrims came to the Holy Monastery, at times from great distances. In the late fourth century, Egeria, a nun from Spain, visited the holy sites in the area and left a vivid written description of her impressions of the small monastery built at the base of the Burning Bush. She also climbed Jebel Musa, where she prayed as she had at the other sacred sites to which the monks led her.

When Egeria visited the Holy Monastery, she described the site as having "many cells of holy men and a church in the place where the [Burning] bush stands, and this bush is still alive today and gives forth shoots." At that time, there were no great walls protecting the church or the Burning Bush. With the small church, there was a tower to which the monks retreated when threatened by the local population or by marauders from the Red Sea. The tower still survives within the Holy Monastery's fortified walls. Most of the monks then lived in separate hermitages spread out around the Holy Monastery's tower and its original church. Today, many of the monks continue to spend time in their private hermitages, where they are able to concentrate on their religious devotions.

According to tradition, the tower and the small church were built for the monks through the generosity of Saint Helena, the mother of Emperor Constantine the Great. She had made an extended pilgrimage to the Holy Land after her son came to power. During her travels, local authorities assisted her in identifying many of the sites—still revered today—where significant events in the life of Christ had occurred, including the Holy Sepulcher. As Saint Helena arranged for the building of Christian churches at the most important of these sites through the influence of her son, the emperor, it is possible that she responded to a request from the monks at Sinai for assistance in building a tower for their defense and a church for their prayers. Certainly, the tower existed by the late fourth century when it is mentioned in the writings of the Egyptian anchorite Ammonios.

Today, as in the time of Egeria, pilgrims come to the Holy Monastery to visit the sacred sites nearby, to see the Burning Bush, and to pray in its church. Now, the path to Jebel Musa starts at the camel station in front of the Holy Monastery where, late at night, people begin the ascent on the relatively broad camel path and finish by climbing the last 750 steps of the Stairs of Repentance. As dawn approaches, the sun's light, extending across the moutain peaks in ever-changing hues, makes them appear to be an endless ocean of frozen waves. On the summit of Jebel Musa is a recent church built largely from the stones of the sixth-century sanctuary located there; a small mosque; and a cleft said to be the one into which Moses retreated as he was exposed to the blinding light of God's glory.

The most direct descent is by the Stairs of Repentance, which were probably built, or finished, in the sixth century. The steep steps, which seem to extend endlessly into the distance, were once the path followed by pilgrims to the summit. Early pilgrims who embarked on the climb were stopped at the Gate of Forgiveness; only after questioning were some deemed properly prepared spiritually to proceed to the top to stand on the holy ground where Moses had appeared shoeless in reverence before God. It is said that for many centuries no one spent the night on the mountain peak out of respect for its sanctity.

Looking closely at the terrain around the mountain paths, it is evident that many creatures—especially birds—and plants thrive in the arid landscape. Near the Holy Monastery, palm and cypress trees flourish. Among the rocks are formations that seem to be imprinted with fossil plants, which some call fossils of the Burning Bush. They are, however, more correctly identified as manganese deposits forming a pattern called dendritic pyrolusite. Quartz crystals also can be found in the region as well as geodes—rocks whose plain surfaces break open to reveal clusters of small quartz crystals.

Another mountain above the Holy Monastery is Jebel Katherina, the highest in the region. It is to this mountain's peak that the body of the princess Catherine is said to have been brought by angels after her martyrdom in Alexandria. The later story of her life, or vita, describes in detail the conversion of the princess to Christianity in the fourth century. Through her learned explanation of the faith, she convinced leading pagan scholars in the city, famed for its literate society, of the virtues of Christianity. When she refused the order of the ruler to repudiate her conversion, he attempted to have her killed on a wheel, which became her attribute. When that failed, he had her beheaded—as depicted on the vita icon displaying scenes of the major events in her life.

As related in her vita, angels carried her body to Jebel Katherina after her death, where, remaining relatively unknown, it was venerated only by local ascetics. In the ninth century, knowledge of the presence of her relics on the mountain became more widespread, and pilgrims began to visit the Holy Monastery in increasing numbers to venerate the saint. During the Middle Ages, Orthodox pilgrims to the Holy Monastery were joined by many from the West, who came to Sinai because of the presence of the relics of Saint Catherine.

Other fourth-century saints are also venerated near the Holy Monastery. There are memorials to the many monks of Sinai and Raitho (modern El Tor), who were martyred in the late fourth century by Saracen invaders. There is also a chapel dedicated to the saints Galaktion and Episteme, a Christian couple, who retreated to Sinai with their followers to spend their lives in devotion before being returned to Alexandria to be martyred for their faith.

The Holy Monastery has produced its own saints as well. Most famous among them is its seventh-century abbot Saint John Climacus, who wrote a set of rules to encourage monks in their search for salvation. His "Heavenly Ladder," with its thirty steps, remains influential for many in the Orthodox Church today. An exquisite Byzantine icon of monks climbing the thirty steps survives at the Holy Monastery, as do depictions of the theme in various manuscripts, including some written in Arabic.

THE HOLY MONASTERY

The Holy Monastery is now named for Saint Catherine, long the most sought after by pilgrims of all the holy figures of the region. Originally, the site was dedicated to the Theotokos, the Mother of God. As the early Church debated the nature of the Virgin and her role in the Life of Christ, the Burning Bush in which God had revealed himself to Moses was used as evidence for the theological position that the Virgin Mary should

The towering southern face of Mount Moses, Jebel Musa.

be called the Theotokos, or Mother of God. The Virgin, like the Burning Bush, had contained God without being destroyed. In the fifth century, the term Theotokos, literally "She who gave birth to God," was officially given to the Virgin. On most icons of the Virgin and Child, that title is displayed alongside the Virgin's head in abbreviated Greek: MP ΘY.

The Holy Monastery's massive walls and the great church are monuments to the pragmatic architecture of the most powerful of the Roman, or Byzantine, emperors ruling from Constantinople: Justinian the Great (r. 527–65). In 330, Constantine the Great had transferred the imperial capital of the Roman Empire to Constantinople on the Bosporus (now Istanbul, Turkey). In the sixth century, Justinian revived the ancient boundaries of the empire to include in his territories most of the Mediterranean Basin as far west as Spain. The Sinai Peninsula on the eastern border of the empire was important to the state for its role in controlling the trade routes between the Indian Ocean and the Mediterranean. It was at that time that the Holy Monastery was transformed into the site as it now exists.

At the request of the monks at Sinai, Justinian ordered the building of a church for those monks who lived at the site— which, by then, had been famous for centuries as the place where the Burning Bush survived—and of a fortress wall to protect the imperial land. Why a location surrounded by mountains was fortified, rather than a mountaintop, is still debated. The presence of the Burning Bush and a stable water source both may have been important in arriving at the deci-

sion. Procopios, the historian of Justinian's building campaigns, recorded that the emperor, at the request of the monks, "raised a church dedicated to the Theotokos . . . not on the mountain's heights, but much further below. . . . at the mountain's foot, the emperor also built a strong fortification, a noteworthy garrison for soldiers to deter the barbarian Saracens who, since the land was desert, passed thither to invade Palestine by stealth."

The Burning Bush survives today within the compound of the Holy Monastery. Botanists have identified the plant as *Rubus sanctus,* a species unique to Sinai, which has an extremely long life, as its root system ensures its perpetual renewal. The Burning Bush now grows in a walled enclosure behind Justinian's church, situated at the heart of the Holy Monastery, although in earlier centuries it may have been planted in an open courtyard behind the church. At the church's entrance is a tall bell tower whose nine bells were the gifts of the Russian czar in 1871, when Sinai, with all the Christians in the Ottoman Empire, was under the protection of the Russian Empire and its Orthodox Church.

Across from the bell tower, one can see the minaret of the mosque that has been housed within the Holy Monastery's walls since the eleventh century. The mosque may have been built in response to Muslim threats at that time. The Holy Monastery has been within Islamic territory since the days of the prophet Muhammad. According to tradition, in 625 the monks sent a delegation to the prophet, who gave them a document promising them security, which he confirmed by his handprint as he could not write. A copy of this document is preserved at the Holy Monastery; the original is said to have been taken to Constantinople to the Ottoman sultan Selim I in 1517. The Ottomans honored the document for the many years that they ruled in Egypt.

Along the walls of the Holy Monastery are multiple buildings, most of which originally served as monks' cells. Many are in near ruin, urgently awaiting restoration. The public entrance to the Holy Monastery is in the south wall of the church. Current visitors arrive and leave via this route to protect as much of the monastic quiet as possible.

Also along the south wall above and beside the entrance is the newly restored Sacristy. Many of the Holy Monastery's greatest treasures are now on display in its secure, climate-controlled, intimate rooms, among them some of the Holy Monastery's most important icons, with their glittering golden grounds; lavishly embroidered textiles; vividly illuminated medieval Byzantine manuscripts; and handsome liturgical vessels; included are works donated to the Holy Monastery by kings and emperors from such diverse countries as France and Russia. Today, heads of state continue to visit the site—the oldest continuously active monastery in the world. Among the recent guests were Charles, Prince of Wales, a patron of the Holy Monastery; the queen of Spain; and Pope John Paul II.

Like all who come to the Holy Monastery, these visitors are shown the well of Moses on its south wall and the pulley by which visitors once gained access to the Monastery, from very early times into the beginning of the twentieth century, when the area was often unstable and the monks at times feared for their lives. During that period, the gates to the Holy Monastery were rarely opened.

The structures on the south side of the Holy Monastery were rebuilt in the early twentieth century. The Monastery's library is located there, and contains one of the greatest collections of Byzantine manuscripts in the world. Many of its masterpieces are now on display in the Sacristy, including leaves from a fourth-century Bible thought to be one of fifty bibles ordered by the emperor Constantine the Great. Much of the manuscript is in the British Library in London, which acquired it from Stalin's Russia after the bible had been given, without willing monastic permission, to Czar Alexander II by the German scholar Konstantin von Tischendorf in 1862. In addition to the Holy Monastery's extensive collection of medieval texts in Greek, its library contains important works in Syriac, Georgian, Armenian, Church Slavonic, Latin, and Arabic—an indication of the Holy Monastery's widespread appeal to Christians throughout the world.

The eastern tower of the Holy Monastery's sixth-century wall and part of its garden. The vast plain of El-Raha opens out in the distance.

Jebel Katherina, where, according to the vita of Saint Catherine, angels brought the body of the saint after her death.

THE CHURCH

The church, one of the most important in the world to have survived from the sixth century, is the heart of the Holy Monastery theologically and physically. It is thought that in Justinian's era one even reached the Burning Bush—then the Monastery's most holy object—through this church. Today, one descends a series of steep steps to enter the simple basilica through a set of medieval inlaid doors. Careful examination reveals that their decoration consists of figures and scenes important to Sinai's association with Moses. In the narthex, the narrow entry room that leads into the church, there is a large image of Saint Catherine set in an intricately carved, eighteenth-century marble frame. More of the many thousands of icons that are housed in the Holy Monastery line the walls.

A pair of monumental wooden doors dating to the sixth century open into the katholikon, or nave, of the church. Inscriptions on the original ceiling beams record that the church was built in the last years of the reign of the emperor Justinian by the local architect Stephanos of Aila. At the far end of the nave is an imposing, gilded eighteenth-century iconostasis, the barrier between the area of the church reserved for the faithful and the semicircular apse reserved for the clergy and the rites of the Eucharist. The present iconostasis, far taller and more ornate than the original one would have been, contains, among its icons, an image of Saint Catherine. The beautiful, elaborately inlaid marble floor is a later addition too—offered, as a gift, by a Christian from Damascus, after the original floor had been destroyed by marauders seeking buried treasure.

In contrast, the monumental columns that separate the katholikon from the side aisles are original to Justinian's building program, as are the chapels that line the side walls of the church. On the left wall, set in a simple wooden niche, is the oldest surviving icon of Saint Catherine with scenes from her life, which shows her dressed as a Byzantine princess. On the columns are medieval calendar icons that depict the saints and the biblical events of each day of the year. More of these important records of the Byzantine calendar survive at Sinai than anywhere else in the world.

Near the midpoint of the katholikon, on the left, is the elaborately decorated proskynetarion, or icon stand. Each day the icon for that day is placed on the stand for veneration by the faithful. Across the nave and located a little further toward the apse is the archbishop's throne. Beautifully carved, it displays on its upright back an image of the Holy Monastery and the sacred sites nearby. Nearer the apse are the lecterns used by the monks for the reading of the services.

Over the centuries, Christians of all persuasions have made donations to the church. Their gifts of icons, lamps, altar furnishings, and other liturgical objects make the church a living expression of the Christian faith, which arrived at Sinai more than seventeen hundred years ago. For example, high up on the walls of the nave are icons that were painted a millennium ago, and below them are equally ancient works as well as some that are recent dedications to the Holy Monastery.

Above and beside the arch of the apse are magnificent sixth-century mosaic images, representative of the finest art of the early Church. Over the apse two angels meet, carrying cross-shaped staffs and cross-decorated orbs. To the left and right are images of Moses: removing his sandals before the Burning Bush and receiving the Tablets of the Law from the hand of God.

Just visible behind the iconostasis is the climax of the mosaic decoration. Covering the vault of the apse, the Metamorphosis (called the Transfiguration in the Western Church) is depicted in stark simplicity against a gold ground, as described in the Gospel of Luke 9: 28–36. At the center, an imposing image of the bearded Christ, garbed in white and gold, stands within a blue mandorla radiating light. At either side of him, and identified by inscriptions, are Elias and Moses, the Old Testament prophets with whom he spoke. At his feet, kneeling in awe and fear, are the disciples John, Peter, and James, who were present at the event. Within medallions surrounding the central image are bust-length representations of the remaining apostles, the evangelists Luke and Mark, Matthias, the major and minor prophets, King David, and a golden cross—the last, positioned over the head of Christ. In one medallion is an image of Longinus, who was abbot of the Holy Monastery at the time that the mosaics were completed.

The walls of the apse are decorated with fine-grained slabs of marble. To the right of the elaborately decorated high altar is the shrine containing the relics of Saint Catherine, which can reached by the chamber to the right of the apse. From the chamber to the left of the apse one can enter the Chapel of the Burning Bush. The chapel, which originally may have been open to the sky, is now roofed. A small altar occupies the niche where the roots of the Burning Bush were once located. The Bush is now found directly behind the chapel in its own enclosure. Blue glazed tiles cover the walls of the intimate chapel, which is sacred to Christians, Jews, and Muslims.

The massive stones at the base of the Holy Monastery's fortified walls are the work of Justinian's builders. The small stones at the top mark the points where, more than 1,200 years later, Napoleon Bonaparte's engineers restored the Holy Monastery's damaged walls after he conquered Egypt in 1801.

ICONS

The thousands of icons that survive at the Holy Monastery are among the greatest treasures of the Orthodox world. When the Orthodox Church rejected the veneration of icons in the eighth and ninth centuries, Sinai was already under Islamic control, and thus the Byzantine state could not force the destruction of its icons. As a result, Sinai possesses the only extant sixth-century icons, including a powerful image of Christ Pantokrator painted in encaustic, a colored melted-wax medium. With the official reinstatement of the veneration of icons in 843, their production flourished throughout the Byzantine world.

Not all the icons at the Holy Monastery were produced there; some were brought to the site. The exceptional quality of a large number of the medieval icons has led to an attempt to associate their center of production with Constantinople, the capital of the Byzantine state. However, others have noted that many of the finest of the icons at the Holy Monastery have burnished gold halos, which are rarely found on icons elsewhere, causing some to suggest that the burnished halos identify a center of icon production at Sinai. As there are icons at the Holy Monastery that represent events specific to its sacred sites, it is tempting to consider those images as works produced at Sinai. One medieval icon depicts Moses before the Burning Bush in a pose closely related to the way in which he is represented in the church's sixth-century mosaic of the same theme. On another icon, Moses appears in the pose of the sixth-century Christ Pantokrator. One of the most compelling icons shows monks seeking salvation on the Heavenly Ladder, an event described by the Sinaitic monk Saint John Climacus.

Icons of Saint George, one of the most popular of the holy warrior saints, were widely known in the Byzantine world. However, it is at Sinai that some of the earliest vita icons are found; in these, the image of a saint is surrounded by narrative scenes of events in the figure's life, focusing especially on those that led to martyrdom and sanctification.

The minaret of the mosque and the bell tower of the church within the Holy Monastery's walls.

the archangels, the guardians of heaven, locates the holy figures in Paradise.

Similarly, the poses of the Virgin and Child in the many images that are found at Sinai also occur on icons throughout the Byzantine world. In keeping with an earlier tradition, the Virgin is often presented sitting erect and formally pointing to her son to show mankind that the way to salvation is through him. This Hodegetria icon type, popular in the medieval period, evolved into increasingly intimate poses of the Virgin and Child. For example, icons of the Virgin Eleousa (or "compassionate," in Greek) often depict Mary with her head bent to touch the cheek of the young Christ, who looks up at her in return. Variants of the theme show the child in even more animated poses. These tender images are meant to encourage the viewer to contemplate the fate of the child, who will sacrifice himself on behalf of mankind. The Virgin's mournful gaze indicates her awareness of his future Passion. The closeness shared by the mother and child is meant to evoke a greater awareness of the pain and sacrifice that is to come.

Many Sinai icons depict the Crucifixion of Christ and the Anastasis (called the Harrowing of Hell in the Western Church). The Anastasis, whose iconography developed in the Byzantine sphere in the medieval period, makes vividly clear the promise of salvation through Christ's death and sacrifice. These images show Christ, who has appeared after his death, descending into hell to rescue Adam and Eve; often, he is represented helping the white-haired couple out of their tombs as he tramples on the gates of hell—or on the devil himself—with the Old Testament kings David and Solomon as well as John the Forerunner (the Baptist) frequently included as witnesses to the event.

Crucifixion icons from the later thirteenth century seen at Sinai often blend traditional Byzantine imagery with motifs adopted from contemporary works made for the Church of Rome. Since the Holy Monastery did not participate in the separation of the Church of Constantinople and that of Rome, which occurred in 1054, this combination of motifs may not have been significant to the Holy Fathers. Instead of depicting Christ attached to the cross with four nails, as is traditional in Byzantine art, in these Crucifixion icons only three nails are visible. The Virgin swoons in grief at Christ's death and angels wail emotionally in the sky over the cross. At times, the inscriptions on the icons are in Latin, not Greek. A number of these works have been identified as having been made for the Crusaders and later Western pilgrims who traveled to Sinai; some icons, such as a painting of Saint Catherine by a Spanish artist, are known to have come from Western sources.

At the northeast corner of the Holy Monastery, a monk is striking a piece of iron to call the monks to the refectory.

Other icons also represent themes common to the Orthodox world. The moving depiction of the archangel Gabriel originally may have been part of a group of icons that showed Christ flanked by the Virgin and John the Forerunner (the Baptist), with archangels in attendance. The grouping of Christ with the Virgin and the Forerunner, who are present as intercessors for mankind, is the popular theme called the Deesis in the Orthodox Church. The presence of

Other icons, however, may be Orthodox images that reflect the complex interconnections between the Orthodox world and the West during the Byzantine Empire's last centuries. It is difficult to determine at whose request the popular Orthodox Syrian military saints Sergios and Bacchos were painted, riding forth brandishing a Crusader flag and carrying a quiver typical of those used by Islamic armies. The richly gilded backgrounds of many of the icons attest to the affluence of the faithful and of the Holy Monastery in the Middle Ages.

THE BEDOUIN

The local Bedouin, by tradition, are thought to be the descendants of the Byzantine soldiers stationed at Sinai in the seventh century. When the region fell to the armies of Islam, the soldiers are said to have converted to the Islamic faith and intermarried with women from local tribes. While the Bedouin of the area have not been Christian for centuries, they have always turned to the abbot of the Holy Monastery to be the judge in their disputes. Also for centuries, the Holy Monastery has provided them with their daily bread. Today, the monks and the Bedouin continue to come together weekly to make bread. Each day, the Bedouin gather at the foot of the Holy Monastery's walls, waiting for those who wish to hire their camels to ascend Jebel Musa. Reverence for Saint Catherine is strong among the Bedouin, and often they are also present at the celebrations of the major feast days at the Holy Monastery.

FEAST DAYS

Pilgrims came—and still come—to the Holy Monastery at all times of the year to worship in the church. The monks celebrate the Divine Liturgy of the Orthodox Church in the early hours of each morning. During the service, the celebrants move back and forth between the katholikon and the apse through the doors in the iconostasis. The monks cense the katholikon and read the service at the lecterns there. Within the apse, the celebrants preparing the Holy Eucharist are visible though the open doors of the iconostasis. As the service proceeds, the dark church slowly fills with the light and warmth of the sun, a powerful daily evocation of the light radiating from Christ in the mosaic in the apse over the altar. At noon, and each afternoon, services are again held in the sixth-century church.

There are twelve great feasts in the Orthodox Church and many more dedicated to specific saints and other events. Certain feasts draw many of the faithful to the Holy Monastery, such as the feast of Saint Catherine, which is celebrated there on December 8. Throngs of pilgrims file through the church for the ceremony. Ranking prelates of the Orthodox world, including the patriarchs of Jerusalem, Alexandria, and Constantinople, are present, along with other leading Church figures from Greece and Cyprus. At the climax of the service, the relics of the saint are carried in procession around the crowded church.

During the Holy Week of Easter, pilgrims take part in the services that commemorate the Resurrection of Christ. On Holy Friday, the Holy Cross is placed in the center of the church. An epitaphios—a large cloth embroidered with an image of the dead Christ—is brought into the church in procession and placed on a table as a symbol of Christ's death and burial. The service on Holy Sunday celebrates his Resurrection: Its icon is the Anastasis, an image that offers all mankind the hope of salvation through Christ's bringing Adam and Eve out of hell.

On January 6, the monks celebrate the Theophany, the manifestation of God, which is called the Epiphany in the West. That day marks the baptism of Christ in the River Jordan by John the Forerunner (the Baptist). The Holy Fathers travel to Orthodox Christian sites by the sea, which have been associated with the Holy Monastery since at least the fourth century. The abbot of Sinai throws a cross into the water and the young men of the region dive in after it, competing to be the first to retrieve it. The joyous celebration is held in honor of the Baptism of Christ.

For more than 1,700 years, the Christian promise of salvation has been celebrated daily at the site of the Burning Bush, where God first appeared to man. Today, under His Eminence Archbishop Damianos of Sinai, and the Holy Fathers, the Holy Monastery continues to flourish—an outpost of Orthodox Christianity, which welcomes those of all faiths within its walls.

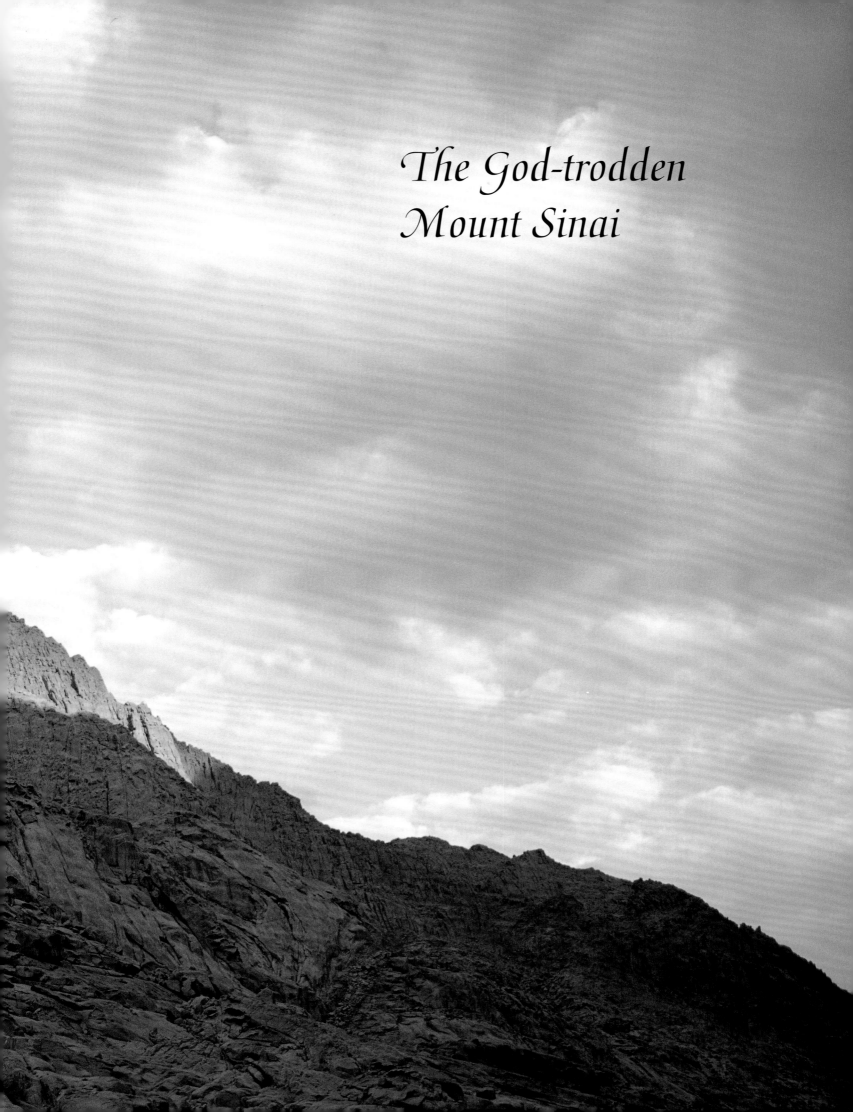

The God-trodden
Mount Sinai

"Moses, Moses, draw not nigh hither: put off thy shoes from off thy feet, for the place whereon thou standest is holy ground" (Exodus 3: 4–5). The barren wilderness of Sinai is the site of God's revelations to the prophet Moses and the children of Israel, and, some six centuries later, to the prophet Elias. From the dawn of the monastic movement, Christian anchorites came to this holy place to devote their lives to prayer and fasting in the harshness of the desert. From the fourth century, pilgrims eager to behold the Holy Mountain of God also made the arduous journey there.

In the fourth century, the nun Egeria wrote, "These mountains are climbed with great difficulty, since you do not ascend them slowly by going round and round, in a spiral path, but you go straight up all the way, as if scaling a wall." By the sixth century, the monks had created a series of steps to aid pilgrims in their ascent. (Left): An ancient hermit's cell near the Church of the Holy Prophet Elias.

(Preceding pages): Ancient paths leading to the Holy Monastery of Saint Catherine (pages 20–21), and sunrise from the upper reaches of Mount Sinai (pages 22–23). (Overleaf): A first glimpse of the Holy Monastery from the Pilgrims' Road (pages 28–29).

(Opposite): To the west of the Holy Monastery is the garden where olives, dates, figs, and other fruits are grown. The church in the center is dedicated to Saint Tryphon, patron saint of gardeners in the Orthodox Church. The bones of the fathers lie below. They rest from their labors, awaiting the day of Resurrection.

(Below): The Archbishop of Sinai shares tea with the Bedouin in a Monastery garden.

Monks and Bedouin kneading and baking bread. The distribution of bread to the Bedouin is a tradition that extends back many centuries and continues to this day.

33

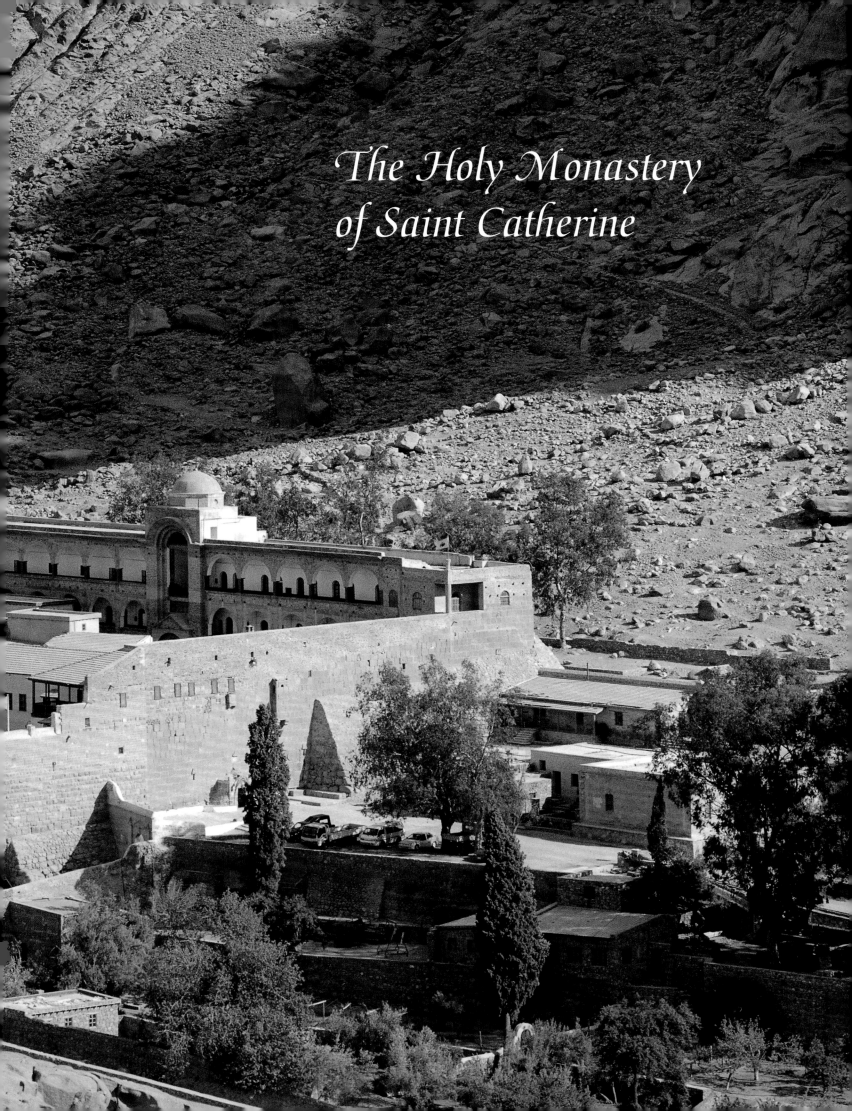

The Holy Monastery
of Saint Catherine

(Above): A monk reposes at twilight on the roof of a
Monastery building overlooking the Sinai's rugged terrain.

(Opposite): The entrance into the Monastery is through walls
built at the command of Emperor Justinian in the sixth century.
These walls are some sixty feet high and ten feet thick. The
entranceway has been adorned with palm fronds and olive
boughs, and with the flags of Egypt and Greece, in preparation
for the feast of Saint Catherine.

(Preceding pages): The sixth-century basilica within the
Holy Monastery's walls.

The bell tower of the Holy Monastery (detail opposite)
dates from the 1870s, and contains nine Russian bells.
These are rung at the beginning of every service, and
during the chanting of the Great Doxology on feast days.
The sound of the bells reverberates through the narrow
valley and may be heard at a very great distance.

(Preceding pages): The Monastery of Saint Catherine is
exceptional in having a mosque next to the church. The ancient
building to the right of the basilica was converted to a
mosque in the early eleventh century, and since then church
and mosque have stood side by side as a symbol of peace.

One thousand years ago, manuscripts were stored in the tower of Saint George (left), but in the eighteenth century they were moved to rooms adjoining the archbishop's quarters (below). Sixteenth-century cells (above) are now reserved for visiting clergy and scholars.

The Holy Monastery is built on a steep incline, so that the various structures are situated on many levels (see above), and, although they date from different periods, they form a harmonious unity. The view at the right shows the flag with a double-headed eagle, the symbol of Byzantium and, later, of the Orthodox Church.

The many activities at the Holy Monastery are all secondary in importance to the daily services held in the basilica. The royal doors at the entrance to the nave are made of cedar of Lebanon wood, and date from the sixth century. Some eight hundred years ago, a pilgrim nailed a Limoges-enamel plaque of Christ in Glory, surrounded by the symbols of the Four Evangelists, to one of the doors, where it has remained to this day (see below).

(Above): A hieromonk in vestments, with pilgrims. Each of the twelve columns in the basilica is adorned with a large icon showing the patron saints for every day of one of the twelve months of the year.

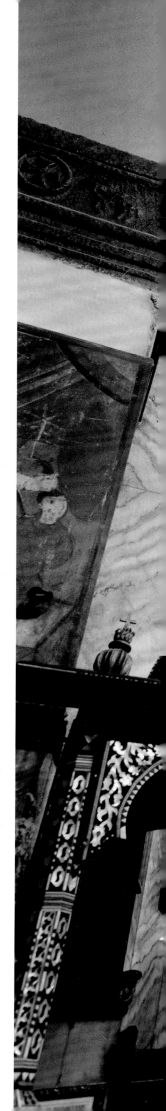

(Right): The incomparable sixth-century mosaic of the Transfiguration of Christ adorns the apse of the basilica.

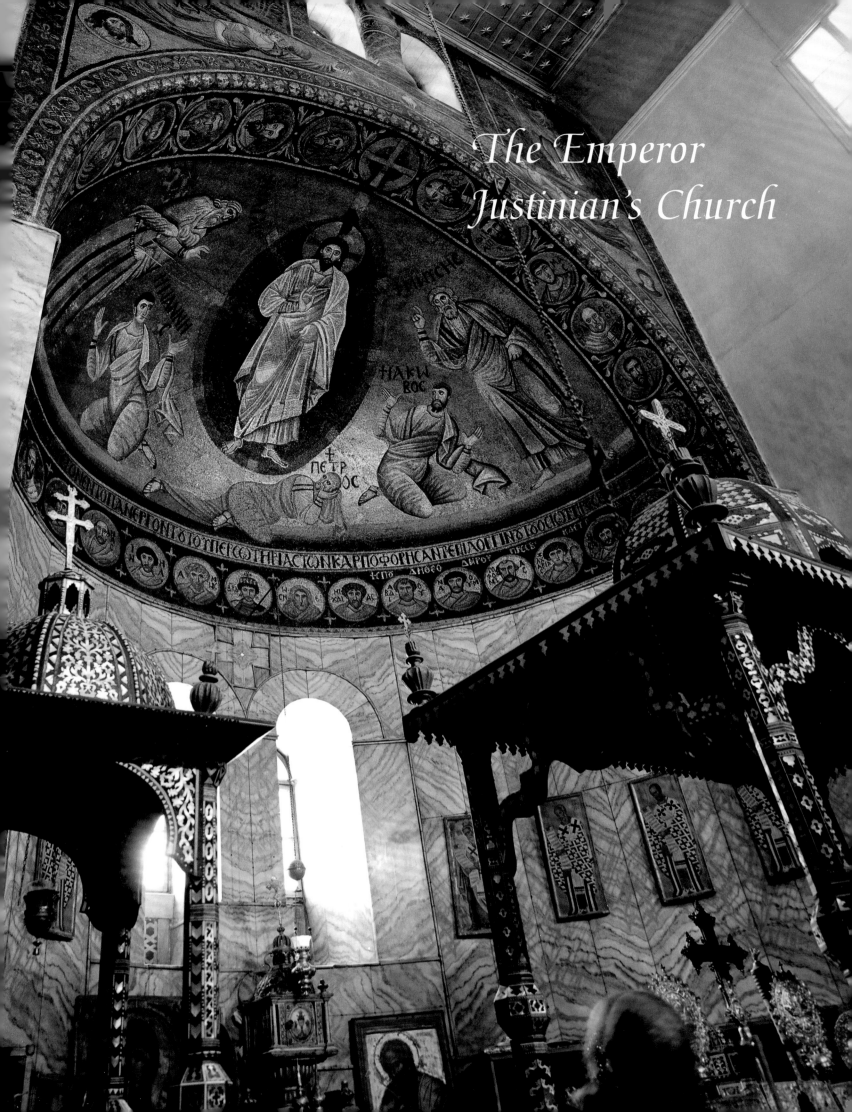

The Emperor
Justinian's Church

Every morning before dawn the service commences. In the spring, as the Divine Liturgy reaches its culmination, rays of light suddenly enter the darkened nave from the highest windows (opposite). Soon after, the entire sanctuary is flooded with sunlight, a palpable reminder of the words from the Paschal homily of Saint John Chrysostom, "Forgiveness hath dawned forth from the tomb," and from the Paschal hymn, "Now are all things filled with light: heaven, and earth, and the nethermost regions of the earth."

Upon entering the church, monks and pilgrims venerate the icon displayed on the proskynetarion (above). In the words of Saint Basil the Great, the honor rendered to the icon ascends to the prototype depicted thereon. (Right): A view of the intricate marble mosaic floor of the church, taken from the sixth-century roof beams.

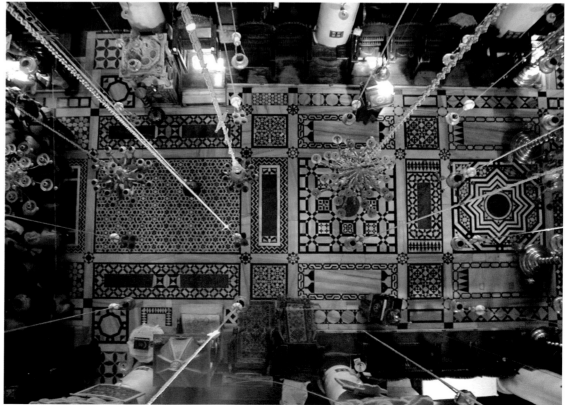

The eighteenth-century
iconostasis spans the front of
the basilica, separating the
sanctuary from the nave. On
the upper tier are icons of the
feast days of the liturgical
year. To the right of the
central gates is an icon of
Christ enthroned as the King
of Kings and Great High
Priest alongside an icon of
Saint Catherine, the bride
of Christ and patron saint of
the Holy Monastery. The
Incarnate Christ, the All-holy
Theotokos, and the saints
unite heaven and earth.

On Friday of Holy Week, the Holy Cross is placed in the center of the church and a table is prepared for the epitaphios, which is embroidered with a representation of Christ prepared for burial. That night, the choirs sing in praise, "Thou, O Life, wast laid in a grave: by Thy death, O Christ, Thou didst destroy death, and Thou didst pour forth life upon the world. . . . Arise, O compassionate One, raising us up also from the depths of Hades."

Nine chapels encircle the great basilica (right). At the Chapel of Saint Marina (above), the proskynetarion enshrines the oldest icon of Saint Catherine, which dates from the thirteenth century and depicts scenes from her life and her martyrdom.

(Opposite): In the first rays of
the morning sun, the mosaic of the
Transfiguration of Christ sparkles
with its brilliance and sublime color.

(Right): In the narthex, pilgrims
have lighted candles before an
icon of Saint Catherine enshrined
in the eighteenth-century carved
marble proskynetarion that once
stood in the apse alongside the
reliquary of the saint.

The nun Egeria described the Burning Bush in the fourth century: "There are many cells of holy men and a church on the spot where the bush stands, and this bush is still alive today and gives forth shoots." The Burning Bush (opposite) has continued to be the subject of descriptions by pilgrims, up to the present day.

"And behold, the bush burned with fire, and the bush was not consumed" (Exodus 3: 2). The eastern chapel of the basilica, the innermost shrine of this great church, is the Chapel of the Burning Bush (above and below); it marks the site of God's revelations to Moses.

The splendor of the basilica (opposite) and of the Chapel of the Burning Bush is in marked contrast to the austerity and simplicity of the other chapels, although all are adorned with icons. The Chapel of Saint James (below), First Bishop of Jerusalem, is situated to the north of the Chapel of the Burning Bush.

These two sixth-century icons, the most famous of those at Sinai, are rare examples of paintings in the encaustic, melted-wax technique. They are surprisingly realistic and, at the same time, supremely spiritual. The apostle Peter (above) is shown holding the keys of the Kingdom in his right hand and in his left hand a staff surmounted by the cross. Christ Pantokrator, Ruler of All (detail, opposite), is depicted with a richly ornamented Gospel book; the icon conveys the compassion of Christ's humanity as well as the authority of his divinity.

Icons:
Images of
the Holy

ΗΑΓΙΑ ΕΚΑΤΕΡΙΝΑ

This icon of Saint Catherine (opposite), which dates from the thirteenth century, presents the saint vested in the robes of a Byzantine princess. Twelve scenes from her life and her martyrdom form the border surrounding the icon.

Painted in Barcelona in 1387, this Gothic-style image of Saint Catherine (right) depicts the saint with her left hand resting on the spiked wheel, the symbol of her martyrdom. In her right hand, she holds the palm of victory.

This twelfth-century icon of the Ladder of Divine Ascent (opposite) illustrates the seventh-century writings of Saint John, Abbot of Sinai. The thirty rungs of the ladder correspond to thirty virtues, and Christ is shown at its summit. Heavenly angels aid the monks in their ascent, while fallen angels test their resolution.

The prophet Moses (above) is shown in this icon raising his right hand in blessing. The scroll in his left hand is inscribed in Greek with the words, "The Lord said."

In this thirteenth-century painting of Moses before the Burning Bush (right), the prophet removes his sandals at God's command.

69

This icon (right) depicts Christ as the Ruler of All. He holds the Gospels open to the page inscribed in Greek with the opening words of the verse "I am the Light of the world: he that followeth Me shall not walk in darkness, but shall have the light of life" (John 8: 12).

Of great beauty and refinement, this large icon of the archangel Gabriel (right) dates to the thirteenth century. In the basilica at Sinai, it hangs opposite the relics of Saint Catherine (see page 86).

Saint George, the courageous general and one of the most beloved saints, is the subject of a monumental icon (opposite) that also includes, around the border, twenty scenes from his life and martyrdom.

Many iconographic details of this double-sided icon, here depicting the Crucifixion, represent a departure from Byzantine iconography, as do the Latin inscriptions. These point to a Crusader provenance and a thirteenth-century date.

This painting of the Resurrection of Christ occupies the reverse side of the icon of the Crucifixion, shown on the opposite page. Holding the cross as a symbol of victory, Christ tramples the gates of Hades, and raises up Adam and Eve from their graves as Death lies captive at his feet.

In this thirteenth-century icon of Saints Sergios and Bacchos (above), martyrs from Syria, the youthful and delicate faces of the saints are set off by the profusion of ornamental details on their weapons and armor.

This icon of the Crucifixion (opposite), painted in the thirteenth century, is one of the most beautiful panels among those icons at Sinai that show a Western influence.

The Enthroned Virgin and Child occupy the center of this icon (opposite), and are surrounded by images of prophets and saints. An icon of profound symbolism, it unites Old Testament vision with New Testament revelation.

This icon of the Virgin Blachernitissa (above) depicts the Virgin Mary raising her hands in prayer, while a bust-length image of Christ in a golden nimbus occupies the space before her. The polished gold circles that adorn the icon are a distinguishing mark of Sinai iconography.

A masterpiece of Late Komnenian art, this twelfth-century icon of the Annunciation (right) includes natural elements in an outdoor setting that reflect the hymn for that feast day, which begins, "Today is the fountainhead of our salvation."

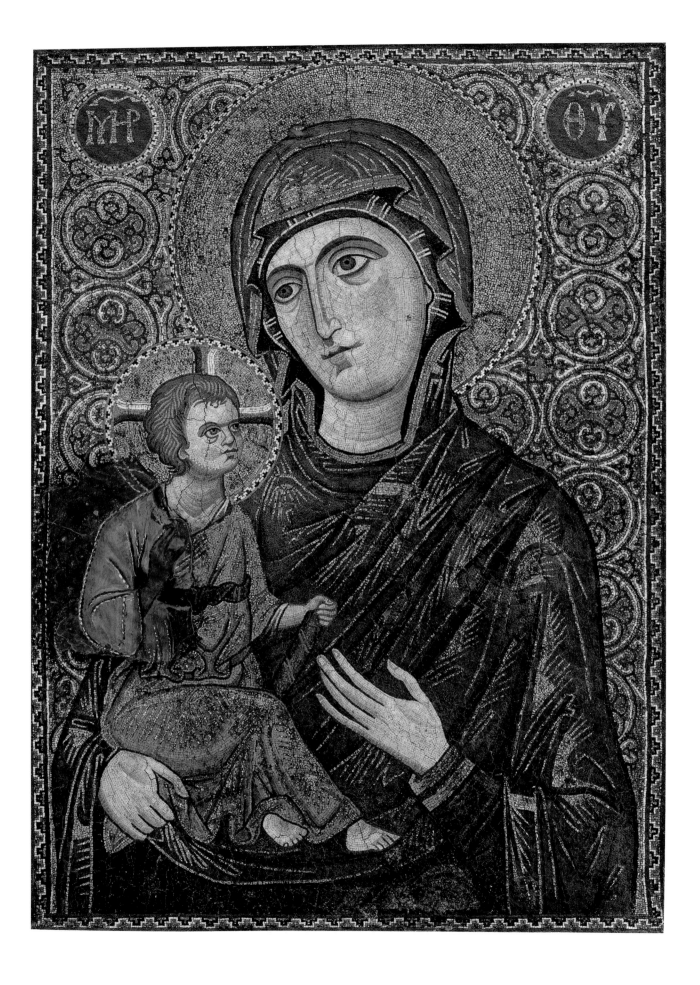

In this icon of the Virgin Pelagonitissa (above), which dates to the fifteenth century, the playful yet tender gesture of the Infant Christ and his lively pose contrast sharply with the serene and reflective expression of the Virgin Mary.

The Virgin Mary and the Infant Christ are depicted in hieratic solemnity in this icon (opposite). The modeling of the forms and the intensity of the color were executed with such sensitivity that only upon close inspection is it apparent that this is a mosaic.

Celebrations of
Great Feasts
of the Church

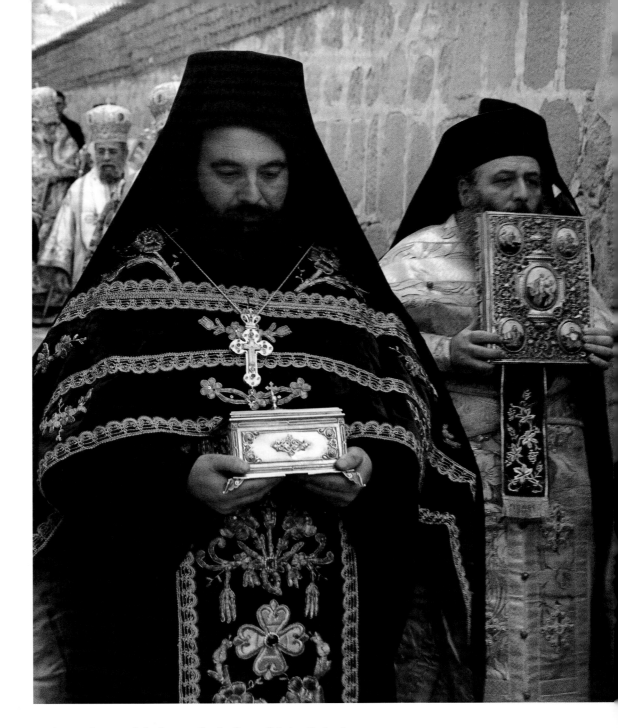

At the conclusion of the liturgy for the feast of Saint Catherine,
the relics of the saint are carried in procession around the
church, and prayers are said at each corner of the basilica to
commemorate the monks of the community and its benefactors,
both the living and those who have gone to their rest: "For all
who have lived according to God's will still live unto God,
though they have departed hence."

For the feast of Saint Catherine, the marble shrine containing her relics is adorned with rich embroideries. Orthodox hierarchs gather from Jerusalem, Alexandria, Greece, and Cyprus for the ceremonies, and the church is filled with a multitude of the faithful.

(Above): Two deacons cense the church, each holding a replica of a church in his left hand. (Right): Archbishop Damianos stands at the kathedra at the beginning of the Divine Liturgy.

Archbishop Damianos celebrates the Divine
Liturgy (left) attended by priests and deacons.
At the end of the long services, a monk
(below) has a cup of coffee at the oikonomeion.

(Overleaf): Blessing holy water
on the feast of the Theophany at
the Monastery's church on the
shore of the Red Sea.

Selected Bibliography

Eckenstein, Lina. *A History of Sinai*. London: Society for Promoting Christian Knowledge; New York: The Macmillan Co., 1921.

Galey, John, *Sinai and the Monastery of St. Catherine*. Introduction by George H. Forsyth and Kurt Weitzmann. Cairo: The American University in Cairo Press, 1985.

Paliouras, Athanasios. *The Monastery of St. Catherine on Mount Sinai*. Sinai: St. Catherine's Monastery, 1985.

Manafis, Konstantinos A., ed. *Sinai: Treasures of the Monastery of Saint Catherine*. Athens: Ekdotike Athenon, 1990.

Hobbs, Joseph J. *Mount Sinai*. Austin: University of Texas Press, 1995.

Baddeley, Oriana, and Earleen Brunner, eds. *The Monastery of Saint Catherine*. Exhib. cat. London: Foundation for Hellenic Culture; London: The Saint Catherine Foundation, 1996.